September 21, 2004

To Jackie & Norm —

Here's hoping these verses
bring you a chuckle or two.
I think you will relate to
quite a few of them. Check out
Page 31, for example.

With very best wishes,

Don Weil

The Older I Get...

LIGHT VERSE FROM A SENIOR PERSPECTIVE

DON WEILL

authorHOUSE

1663 LIBERTY DRIVE, SUITE 200
BLOOMINGTON, INDIANA 47403
(800) 839-8640
www.authorhouse.com

First published by AuthorHouse 05/28/04

ISBN: 1-4184-0973-1 (e)
ISBN: 1-4184-0975-8 (sc)
ISBN: 1-4184-0974-X (hc)

Library of Congress Control Number: 2004090891

Printed in the United States of America
Bloomington, Indiana

This book is printed on acid-free paper.

Designed by Jessica Venegas.

DEDICATION

For Elaine

CONTENTS

PREFACE

I find it hard to believe that the poems in this collection of senior-oriented verse were written over a period of 40 years. The earliest, "The Reluctant Investor," originally appeared in *Realty* in 1964 and was included in my book, <u>The Reluctant Investor and Other Light Verse</u>, published in 1977. I was not a senior citizen way back then. Not even middle-aged. But the poem was written from a senior citizen perspective and so it is included in this volume.

While most of these light verse pieces were created in the last few years, some saw the light of day in every decade from the '60s on. This will explain why reference is made to my daughter of 19 ("Full Circle"), 28 ("Mixed Blessing") and 46 ("Relativity"). Don't be confused. Each was written at a different stage of her life and of mine.

It is impossible to be a writer and not be influenced by that which came before. As I wrote in the poem "Remember Babylonia" in a somewhat different context: "Every generation builds upon the wisdom of the past…" Therefore, I confess from the outset that I have built some of these efforts upon the works of poets far better known and far more talented than I. As an example, the opening line in the poem "The Negotiator" is a word-for-word lift from A.E. Housman"s "Loveliest of Trees," the second poem in his great "A Shropshire Lad" collection.

I am doubly indebted to John Greenleaf Whittier: first, for his famous concluding lines, and second, for his basic theme concerning life's missed opportunities. My poem "The Reluctant Investor," which ends with, "If only I'd invested then," derives from Whittier's "Maud Muller" with its famous plaint, "For of all sad words of tongue or pen/ The saddest are these: 'It might have been!'" Another of Whittier's famous poems, "The Barefoot Boy," echoes lightly in the third stanza of "Lost at the Beach."

The poem, "Obsolescence," is beholden to Oliver Wendell Holmes' "The Last Leaf." It describes an ancient veteran of the Revolutionary War, bent with age, still walking the streets of Boston in his old three-cornered hat in 1832, the year the poem was published. My central character in "Obsolescence" is also far past his glory years. Further, the structure of both poems is somewhat similar with truncated lines ending each stanza.

The title of my nostalgic effort, "Where Are the Toys of Yesteryear?" derives from the 15th Century poem by Francois Villon, "Where Are the Snows of Yesteryear?"

Finally, William Wordsworth's "The Rainbow" contains the classic line: "The child is father of the man" and that line was father to my country-western lyric included herein: "You've Got to Keep the Boy in the Man." Two others, incidentally, which started their lives as song lyrics are "Poof!" and "Where Are You, Sue Ann?"

Since confession is good for the soul, I must confess that my soul feels thoroughly cleansed for having confessed to my "pilferage" of words and ideas from Housman, Holmes, Whittier, Villon and Wordsworth. I believe that these five represent the lot of them except perhaps for a definition of old age from Bernard Baruch which I gleaned from Roget's Thesaurus for use in "Park Bench Philosopher." In all fairness, that quotation – "Old age is 15 years older than I" should probably not be included. What is a thesaurus for if it is not to serve as a source for a writer's writings? That same quotation, incidentally, is the title for an enjoyable collection of quotations regarding growing older put together by Randy Voorhees and published by Andrews McMeel a few years back.

The question of giving credit where it is due cuts both ways, of course. My poem "The Reluctant Investor," has been reprinted worldwide, more often than not attributed to "Anonymous" or "Author Unknown." In fact, an author who had incorporated "The Reluctant Investor" in a book of his which sold more than 1,000,000 copies, called me one day after learning the error of his ways. He had seen my poem in many places over many years and figured it must be in the public domain. His opening remark to me was: "It's nice to know you're still alive."

I couldn't have agreed with him more. That conversation took place some fifteen years ago. Not much has changed. It's still nice to be alive…

Westfield, New Jersey
February 24, 2004

WHO? WHAT? WHEN? WHERE?

I showed up at a restaurant
And how my panic grew!
I had a date with someone, but
Could not remember WHO.

I came into my living room,
Stood frozen to a spot,
I'd come there for some reason, though
I couldn't tell you WHAT.

I lost my theater tickets,
It happens now and then.
They asked which day we're going,
I couldn't tell them WHEN.

I laid aside my glasses,
They vanished in thin air.
I'm sure they're with the others,
But I am clueless WHERE.

I'm frazzled by these questions,
By all they may imply,
Forget about WHO, WHAT, WHEN, WHERE…
The question now is WHY.

LOST AT THE BEACH

When I was but a youngster
I knew of no more fun
Than heading for the seashore
And soaking up the sun.

With no protective lotion
To block the sun's bright rays
I frolicked by the ocean
In bygone summer days.

That carefree lad has vanished
That boy with cheek so tan
And in his place you find me,
A very cautious man.

I'm under an umbrella
I'm sun-screened head to toe
I'm wiser, yes, but duller
Where did the old me go?

A youngster shouts, "Hey, mister!"
His beachball's rolled my way
I pick it up and toss it back
To him…and yesterday.

THE NEGOTIATOR

Of my three score years and ten,

None of them will come again.

Today the least I'll settle for

Is, let us say, a dozen more

And when I reach age eighty-two,

I figure even that won't do

So, subject to how well I feel

I'll renegotiate the deal

By adding one more point worth mention:

Another twelve-year life extension.

Not a bad deal, I agree,

After that, we'll see…we'll see…

MOODSWING

My 30th birthday came and went, soft as a summer breeze.
When "life began at 40," I was totally at ease.
At 50, my half-century mark, I had myself a ball,
And all those years that end in "5" had no effect at all.
So, how to explain the moodswing that was added to the mix,
That suddenly came over me when I turned 56?
Somber was my state of mind, sullen was my soul,
I had this feeling deep inside that I had lost control.
Worried about life's meaning, caught in a web of fear,
For now that I'd turned 56, I sensed the end was near.
Oppressed by time, in need of space, I left the house at dawn,
My wife was still asleep and had no clue that I was gone.
My daughter and my sons? There was no way that they
      could know,
The last of them had left the nest some eighteen months ago.
Down random residential streets I wandered in the dark,
My steps took me, unconsciously, through Tamawaskin Park.
Its silent swings, its ballfields where my children used to play
"So long ago, so long ago," the silence seemed to say.
At Fairview Cemetery on the eastern edge of town
I paused to let its message drive my spirits further down.
The churches and the synagogue for which our town
      is known,

All meant to elevate the soul, did nothing for my own.
The firehouse and the movie house and all the stores on Main
Went virtually unnoticed by my mood-infected brain.
By then the sky was brightening which seemed to coincide
With nature's call and hunger pangs that could not be denied.
I quickly turned my steps toward home. My wife stood at
      the door,
There was a look upon her face I'd never seen before.
My lips were poised to let her know the mood that I was in,
Instead, she interrupted me with: "Grandpa, where've
      you been?"
"Grandpa!" What was that about? My daughter wasn't due,
I vaguely recollected, for another month or two.
Impatient to embrace his world, the child had jumped the gun
And just like that, my somber mood was over, dead and done.
I've never had a moodswing such as I had on that day,
But, I've had five more grandkids, and two more are on
      the way.
As for birthdays, since that morning they don't bother me
      at all,
And that boy who shares my birthday leaves for college in
      the fall.

ROLE MODEL

Watch that old guy hit the ball!

Watch that old guy run!

They told me at the tennis shack

That old guy's ninety-one!

I hope that in the book of life

I find that old guy's page

So I can learn to play like him

When I'm that old guy's age.

FULL CIRCLE

When my daughter was a youngster,
She believed that I was king,
That the scope of Daddy's wisdom
Encompassed everything.

When my daughter reached her teen years,
I must have grown quite dense,
Each opinion that I offered her
Made not the slightest sense.

But of late I'm getting smarter,
(My daughter's turned nineteen.)
Now I'm neither dolt nor genius,
But something in between.

At the rate that I'm improving,
If all should go by plan,
By the time my daughter's thirty,
I'll be back where I began.

SHHH...

It happens more and more these days
Now that I'm growing older,
A subway ride oft finds my head
Upon a stranger's shoulder.

Were I awake, I would explain
Why I'm in that position
And hope that he would understand
My sleep-deprived condition.

I'd urge that stranger not to shout
Or punch or kick or bite me,
But, simply shift his weight toward mine
And, in that manner, right me.

Or, better still, just let me be
Until my destination,
Then, gently wake me from my dreams
At Pennsylvania Station.

I'D LIKE YOU TO MEET...

I see him among all the others

And ought to go over I know.

We two were both classmates and brothers

A hundred or more years ago.

We gravely vowed friendship eternal

Through failure or fortune or fame

And I would be fiercely fraternal

Could I but remember his name.

THE LONG AND SHORT OF IT

When I am feeling in the pink,

I'll live to 99, I think,

But when my forehead's burning hot,

A week, I fear, is all I've got.

My life expectancy, it seems,

Lies in between these two extremes.

To state my preference in the matter:

I'll take the former—not the latter.

DOCTOR, NO SURPRISES, PLEASE

My yearly physical exam
Is now at hand, so here I am,
Ill-at-ease in the waiting room
With time to contemplate my doom,
And, frankly, I'm in no great hurry,
I need sufficient time to worry
About these fears I can't avoid
(Now don't tell me I'm paranoid!)
When someone's seven decades old
Most any ailment can take hold,
For instance, this new floating pain
Is no mere figment of my brain.
I want to know if it will pass,
A threat to life or simply gas?
And now that I've reached senior league,
Why do I feel this deep fatigue?
Does my desire for frequent naps
Portend my journey's end, perhaps?
The tests I took three days ago?
God only knows what they will show,
PSA and EKG?
Will they unveil what's ailing me?
Bloodwork? Urinalysis?
To think my life depends on this!

Last year my systems, on the whole,
Were under pretty tight control.
There was that spike in my albumin
Which only proved that I was human,
But, by and large, I must admit
I have been feeling fairly fit,
Though I recall some friends of mine
Who figured they were doing fine
Learned on a morning such as this
Some vital signs had gone amiss,
That they'd been hit by something bad
They never would have dreamed they had.
With thoughts like these I vacillate
While gloomily I sit and wait
Until the nurse's voice I hear
As if from some far-distant sphere.
It penetrates my brain somehow:
"Dr. Becker will see you now."
Chin up, eyes forward, shoulders back,
I, Hero Hypohchondriac,
Pass through the same familiar door
Which I've passed through so oft before
To do what I'm supposed to do,
To take deep breaths, to cough on cue,
To feel the mallet on my knees,
To suffer gross indignities,
My hate for which lies in between
The gallows and the guillotine.

At long last the exam is done
(How time does fly when you're having fun!)
Now all I really want to know
Is if my status stayed at "quo,"
That there's no red-flagged warning sign
On all those lab reports of mine.
In short, I simply want to hear:
"You're doing fine. See you next year."
But I'm left hanging by my thumbs
While Dr. Becker reads…and hums,
He then looks up, about to speak—
My mouth goes dry, my legs grow weak
And my one prayer at times like these
Is, "Doctor, no surprises, please."

WHERE ARE THE TOYS OF YESTERYEAR?

Where are the toys of yesteryear...
The Toonerville trolley from that bygone time?
The hobby-horse with the missing ear?
The battalion of soldiers from the five-and-dime?

Where are the Lionel trains of yore?
The jack-in-the-box and the Tonka truck?
Those alphabet blocks on the bedroom floor?
The Mickey Mouse windup? The Donald Duck?

For me they remain but a memory today,
Those toys I demolished or simply outgrew;
With total indifference, I tossed them away,
But, hey! I was only a kid then. Who knew?

What's gone is gone. Yes, that's a lesson I've learned,
But, in truth, it's no reason for tears,
For if I could choose to have something returned,
It would be not the toys, but the years.

TWO NOSES PRESSED AGAINST
THE NURSERY WINDOW

My son-in-law's dad is deluded, I think,

Or maybe addicted to drugs or to drink.

Perhaps what might pass for his brain has grown dim,

He thinks that this grandson we share looks like him.

It's barely an hour since my daughter gave birth

To – clearly – the handsomest baby on earth

And anyone who's in his right mind can see

The child is the absolute image of me.

Don't you agree?

THE RELUCTANT INVESTOR

I hesitate to make a list
Of the countless deals I've missed,
Bonanzas that were in my grip,
I watched them through my fingers slip,
The windfalls that I should have bought
Were lost because I overthought.
I thought of this, I thought of that,
I could have sworn I smelled a rat,
And while I thought things over twice,
Another bought them at the price.
It seems I always hesitate,
Then make my mind up much too late.
A very cautious man am I
And that is why I never buy.

When tracks rose high on Sixth and Third,
The prices asked I felt absurd,
Whole blockfronts — bleak and black with soot —
Were priced at thirty bucks a foot!
I wouldn't even make a bid,
But others did — yes, others did!
When Tucson was cheap desert land,
I could have had a heap of sand;

When Phoenix was the place to buy,
I thought the climate much too dry;
"Invest in Dallas — that's the spot!"
My sixth sense warned me I should not.
A very prudent man am I
And that is why I never buy.

How Nassau and how Suffolk grew!
North Jersey! Staten Island, too!
When others culled those sprawling farms
And welcomed deals with open arms —
A corner here, ten acres there
Compounding value year by year,
I chose to think and as I thought
They bought the deals I should have bought.
The golden chances I had then
Are lost and will not come again.
Today I cannot be enticed
For everything's so overpriced.
The deals of yesteryear are dead;
The market's soft — and so's my head!

Last night I had a fearful dream,
I know I wakened with a scream;
Some Indians approached my bed —
For trinkets on the barrelhead
(In dollar bills worth twenty-four
And nothing less and nothing more),

They'd sell Manhattan Isle to me.
The most I'd go was twenty-three.
The Indians scowled: "Not on a bet!"
And sold to Peter Minuit.

At times a teardrop drowns my eye
For deals I had, but did not buy
And so, life's saddest words I pen:
"If only I'd invested then!"

DISJOINTED

I join in saluting the surgical arts
And applaud what those surgeons have done!
They've learned to replace all our moveable parts,
Their talents are second to none.

Should you need a shoulder, a finger, a hip,
An ankle, an elbow, a knee,
Your good-natured neighborhood orthopedist
Is surely the fellow to see.

While working with plastic of medical grade,
Stainless steel and titanium, too
He will fashion a joint that's a perfectly-made
Replacement for that part of you.

Take note, I said "you," for if push comes to shove,
It's my body (I've had quite a run with it).
So, instead of new parts, here's what I'm thinking of:
Simply clone all of me and be done with it.

CALL ME SIR

The next time a waiter who's one-third my age

Chooses to call me "young fella,"

I'll give vent to my rage and dent his rib cage

With my fist or perhaps my umbrella.

I'll shanghai that callous and unthinking clown

(Whose wretched remark really rankles)

To some tower in town where he'll hang upside-down

While I'm holding tight to his ankles.

Then, after somewhere between two hours and three

And provided I've not lost my grip —

I'll set the fool free, but I guarantee

From me he's not getting a tip.

WATCHING THE SUN

When I first retired — I have to admit —
I missed the old rat race, more than a bit.
I cherished the teamwork, the goals and the feel
Of triumph that comes after closing a deal.
Back then it was pressure that kept me alive.
I knew only one business gear — overdrive.

But as I grew older, I resented the grind,
Or, perhaps I'd slowed down; that thought entered
     my mind,
For time has a way of exacting its toll
Which, in part, might explain my retirement role.
With time for reflection, I realize this—
So much of that old life I know I won't miss:

No time-wasting meetings, no racing for planes,
No plowing through statements of losses and gains,
No rising at dawn for the morning commute,
No spending my days in a dark business suit,
No sweating out payrolls, the bane of my life,
Today I intend to have lunch with my wife.

No soothing the feathers of employees upset,
No desperate deadlines that have to be met,
No memos marked "urgent" which are anything but,
No everyday tensions to tie up my gut,
No grief from conditions beyond my control,
This morning I may smell that rose on my stroll.

My schedule is now what I want it to be,
Busy or lazy – it's all up to me.
I can take some golf lessons, shave strokes off
          my score,
Join twenty-five organizations or more,
Or mentor one youngster – a man could do worse –
Oh, yes – and I might try my hand at light verse.

I know that my life is no longer a race
For the longer I live, the slower the pace.
Here in retirement, I do as I choose,
Take a class in the morning, take an
          afternoon snooze,
And evenings, I guess, the one thing I do best
Is watching the sun as it sets in the west.

JACKPOT FANTASY

It would mean a lot to me,

Pure joy would fill my cup,

If I could win the lottery

Before my number's up.

A STAR TOO FAR

When young, I was told

To follow my star,

I tried to, but stopped in a day

When I realized

The star that I prized

Was two million light years away.

It wasn't the going

That boggled my mind

And made me stop cold in my track,

But the question arose

How did they propose

That I was supposed to get back?

THE JOKE

Perhaps you've heard the joke about

The two old men on a park bench, sunning.

One s-l-o-w-l-y rises, limps off, groans,

His friend calls out: "So, where you running?"

Oh, how I laughed! Now, my reaction's

About as different as day from night is,

I feel his pain — and that's a fact —

Since I have come to know arthritis

Whose visit caught me unaware.

Now I rise s-l-o-w-l-y from my chair.

My joints aren't what they used to be.

These days, I guess, the joke's on me.

MAYBE

Maybe it comes by email
Maybe a voice on the phone
Maybe she hears from a friend of a friend
That an old flame's now living alone.

It's a few years since she lost her husband,
Maybe two years since he lost his wife,
But one thing's for certain, no maybes about it,
It's time she got on with her life.

They each may have two or three children
And likely some grandchildren, too.
Maybe she wonders what they would be thinking
If she took up with somebody new.

Maybe she pictures him clearly
Maybe her memory is dim
Maybe the yearbook she found in her attic
Contains an old photo of him.

His suggestion that they get together
Has thrilled her yet filled her with dread.
What changes in him has a half century wrought?
Does he still have some hair on his head?

And, maybe, while still on the subject
Of changes that surely occur
With the passage of time, then what of the changes
That time has bestowed upon her?

Maybe her fervor has dwindled,
No need to ask where it went
But with someone to love, could that fire be rekindled
To a greater or lesser extent?

Maybe she's known other women
Who are suddenly part of a pair,
Who smile all the time from the joy they are feeling,
Who seem to be floating on air.

Maybe her positive feelings
Always seem riddled by doubt
But now that they've spoken, she's bound and determined
To see how the whole thing works out.

After all, what's the worst that could happen?
It won't work and she'll shed a few tears.
She's shed plenty of those, but maybe, just maybe,
He'll be hers for the rest of her years.

Maybe there's the sound of the doorbell
Maybe a knock at the door
Maybe her hand shakes as she turns the doorknob.
Soon enough she'll know what lies in store.

Maybe...

NEVER TOO LATE

When old folks

Find new romances,

It restores one's faith

In second chances.

PARK BENCH PHILOSOPHER

Bernard Baruch, it cannot be denied,

Was an extremely intelligent guy.

When asked "What is old age?" wise Bernard replied:

"It's fifteen years older than I."

ME AND THE COSMOS

It took me a lifetime of scanning the sky,
Staring into the infinite void,
In abject humility, I would ask "What am I?"
I admit I was deeply annoyed.

A great revelation has now set me free,
Shown me my appropriate place,
Let the universe see here stands little ol' me
Smack dab in the center of space.

I don't like to boast, yet if it's a fact
That the cosmos is utterly boundless,
Forgive me the smugness with which I react,
But humility's got to be groundless.

Were you to declare that the center is you,
It would not cause my bubble to burst,
The fact is your claim's universally true,
But remember...I thought of it first.

I HAD A MID-LIFE CRISIS

I had a mid-life crisis

It seemed the thing to do

Since all my friends were having one

I had to have one, too.

I had a mid-life crisis

And I survived the blow

The details? Who remembers?

It was thirty years ago.

Thanks to that mid-life crisis

I'm well-prepared today

Should ever a late-life crisis

Chance to come my way.

THERE'LL BE A SHORT WEIGHT

I must purchase a new bathroom scale,

For now that I'm older I've found

My present device is a bit too precise

As it notes each superfluous pound.

If there's one thing I do not require,

It's the honest machine that I've got.

I'm going to buy a digital liar

To skim a few pounds from the pot.

GRANDPA WASN'T BORN THIS WAY

Grandson, it's not nice to chuckle
As I struggle from my seat,
Burp, then loosen my belt buckle
As if I've had too much to eat.
Overeating's not the question,
At your age I ate much more.
But I have chronic indigestion.
That's what Pepto Bismol's for.

I know it isn't too endearing,
Me repeating, "Say again?"
I'll admit I'm hard of hearing,
Which I wasn't way back then.
Grandson, though my body's sagging,
Pace is dragging, hair's turned gray,
Though my energy keeps flagging,
Grandpa wasn't born this way.

Just to prove that I'm not fooling,
Here's a book of photographs:
That baby on the bear rug, drooling,
Is really me. I knew you'd laugh.
Here I'm sitting on a pony.
Here my bike is shiny new.

Here my face is testimony
To how much I looked like you.

Here's a young girl cheering wildly
Shouting through her megaphone.
I worshipped her, to put it mildly,
The Grandmother I wish you'd known.
Understand life comes in stages,
Changing every time you look.
Boy, you're on the early pages
In life's ever-changing book.

Of the years in my possession,
I've watched cycles come and go.
I lived through the Great Depression
And wars I pray you'll never know.
Do you think that Grandpa landed
On this earth as I look now?
It took years, to be quite candid,
For me to earn my wrinkled brow.

I suppose I shouldn't bother
Telling you all this today;
You'll know when you're some boy's grandfather
That Grandpa wasn't born this way.

MIXED BLESSING

The year my wife attained the age

My daughter reached today,

My daughter was a five-year-old,

My son was on the way.

My father had a granddaughter

To bounce upon his knee,

While I've a 28-year-old

Who has her law degree.

WHERE ARE YOU, SUE ANN?

I came to Fort Knox out of Fort Benning, Georgia
And when the week's drilling was through
I drove to a Louisville club called the Snake Pit,
That's where I first danced with you.

From our very first step, from that very first moment,
We both knew what fate had in store,
So, night after night on the old Dixie Highway
I drove from Fort Knox to your door.

You made my last months in the States seem like heaven,
Lost darling, you sure aimed to please,
Then one day my orders came through and we parted,
Those orders sent me overseas.

I came back from war, got a job, raised a family,
Grew older, my hair's turned to gray.
There are times when I think I should pay you a visit,
But I won't — and it's better that way.

Where are you, Sue Ann, and what are you doing
And what kind of hand has life dealt you, Sue Ann?
Long years have gone by since the last time I saw you,
I still see you clearly, Sue Ann.

The years in between haven't faded my memory,
There are times when I whisper your name,
While everything else in my life keeps on changing,
You remain ever the same.

AS TIME GOES BY

I am amazed by the passage of time,

Life races by in a blur.

We aren't as young as we used to be,

How weird it would be if we were.

THE DOCTORS WILL SEE YOU NOW…

Friends and acquaintances ebb and flow

Sometimes they come; more often they go

But the numbers stay constant…and why is this so?

The older I get, the more doctors I know.

REMEMBER BABYLONIA

In this age of transplantations, cybernetics and men's feet
Treading lightly on the moon's disfigured face,
When this morning's innovations are this evening obsolete,
Who can say that demolition's a disgrace?

So, to you who loved Penn Station and the Roxy and the Met
And to you who called the Ritz your second home,
Pray, remember Babylonia, Colossus ne'er forget,
Nor the dim and distant glory that was Rome.

Did the Hippodrome's destruction toll a sad, nostalgic bell?
Was Klein's among your dear departed friends?
Did you feel yourself grow older when the Singer
        Building fell,
Though you know full well that what goes up, descends?

Ebbets Field no longer echoes to the shouts that mark
        the game,
The old Astor and the Capitol are down,
And the Savoy's but a memory, the Ziegfeld's but a name
In the endless reconstruction of this town.

As man's knowledge keeps compounding from an ever-
        broadening base
And his swelling numbers pose a growing threat,
Older structures will be razed at an accelerating pace
And it's obvious we ain't seen nothin' yet.

Bid farewell to all those faded prints of Currier & Ives,
For the book of life's an evoluting text,
If you flip the pages quickly, all the structures of our lives
Can be caught between this eyeblink and the next.

When they tear down Lincoln Center, when the New York
        Hilton goes,
When the Seagram Building feels the wrecker's ball,
I'll be watching with my grandson who at ten already knows
That he'd better hold me fast for fear I'll fall.

When One Chase Manhattan Plaza is torn down and
        borne away,
I suspect the boy will yawn (while I feel faint),
But I'll summon all my energy and make him dearly pay
If he has the gall to call that tower "quaint."

When the demolition of the Pan Am Building has begun,
I assure you I'll be fully reconciled
With that youngster on my arm ...(Is he Steve or
        Wendi's son?
Is it possible he's Jeff or Kenny's child?)

That the World Trade Center may one day become the
      sprawling site
For a newer center seven times as tall
Doesn't bother me, for progress is as sure to come as night
And I pledge to feel no pangs of guilt at all.

Every generation builds upon the wisdom of the past
As the torch of life is handed down the years,
Our most visible creations are not guaranteed to last.
No, the fall of buildings leads me not to tears.*

But the vision of that youngster yet unborn who tugs
      my sleeve
Has me mistier than any building can;
Mankind's legacy is not the passing structures that we leave,
It's the boundless, seeking, soaring dreams of man.

*NOTE: I was wrong. On October 5, 2001, flying northward
out of Newark Airport, bound for Boston and my son Kenny's
wedding, our plane passed close to the still-smoldering World
Trade Center site. Yes, tears were shed.

THE HAMMOCK

Lazy June – the birds are singing,

I see a hammock that can use some swinging,

All it needs is a body in it,

I'll be there in half a minute.

MUSINGS OF AN AGING ATHLETE

Someone, someone, tell me, please,
Where did I get these aching knees?
Please explain, ere I grow older,
This nagging pain in my left shoulder.
Because of my arthritic joints,
I lose too many tennis points.
At golf, my torn rotator cuff
Is why my ball lies in the rough.
It seems the gods of pain don't like me,
They lie in wait and then they strike me.
First my neck and then my back
Are hapless targets of attack.
Why is it when one pain departs,
It's guaranteed another starts?
Oh, I have weapons of my own
Like ibuprofen, cortisone,
Celebrex and Vioxx, too,
And let's give aspirin its due.
But, mild pain-killers such as these
Are temporary remedies
And I don't choose, if you don't mind,
To try the everlasting kind.
So, weighing the alternative,
With all my pains I'll gladly live

Aware of old friends I could name
No longer here to play the game.
That sobering thought brings me up short,
And so, while still involved in sport,
I'll heed these words which say it all:
"Quit complaining! Hit the ball!"

RX FOR MDS

Of my many doctors

I do not ask a lot.

If I'm okay

Keep me that way...

Or cure me today if I'm not.

NOT MY FATHER'S MUSTACHE

This morning I shaved off my mustache,
A grievous mistake, it appears,
It had lived in repose
'Twixt my lip and my nose,
My companion for 42 years.

But I'd wanted to know what I looked like
I yearned for the pure barefaced truth
Would I know the me
That I used to be,
Way back in my pre-mustache youth?

My onslaught with scissor and razor
Caused me deep emotional pain,
With each razor stroke
My heart well-nigh broke
As my whiskers were washed down the drain.

I gazed at the face in the mirror
With feelings I cannot define
For my father's face
Had taken the place
Of the face that I thought to be mine.

I loved and admired my father,
But never thought we looked the same,
Yet mirrors don't lie,
We were one, he and I,
In appearance as well as in name.

I realize time brings on changes,
Slow and steady as people mature,
So, it wasn't too strange
That my features would change,
A fact that my mustache obscured.

But now to face up to the problem,
And not leave my life in a lurch,
I vow that I will
Hide my razor until
My mustache returns to its perch.

BASIC MATHEMATICS

It's hard to deny that which appears

To be a self-evident fact:

Youngsters prefer to add to their years,

Oldsters prefer to subtract.

DIALOG

"Enlighten us, dear Widow Brown,
Why do you wear that longish frown?"

"They want to buy the property
Sam, my husband, left to me."

"That lemon!—Beg your pardon, ma'am,
I meant the property—not Sam."

"Those builders never understood
How much it warms my widowhood."

"Few things are 'warmer' here on earth
Than grabbing twice your building's worth."

"I hardly paid attention to
The price they offered me, did you?"

"Eight hundred thousand dollars net!
A price you never dreamed you'd get."

"Eight hundred is a tidy bit...
But, no, I mustn't think of it."

"I guess they'd go a hundred more,
Your building's where they want their door."

 "What's money? When it's spent, it's spent.
 They've no regard for sentiment."

"I've never seen a love so true.
How would an even million do?"

 "Young man, I haven't got all day—
 Let's close before they get away!"

"Enjoy Jamaica, Widow Brown,
And call me when you're back in town."

 "I'm sure my Sam will have a fit.
 Oh, well, he'll learn to live with it."

STRUNG OUT

I used to tie a string around my finger

Which functioned as an ever-faithful clue,

So, when I woke and saw it in the morning,

I knew exactly what I had to do.

Older now, when I wake in the morning

And see a string, I'm driven to despair;

Puzzled why that string is on my finger,

Curious who might have tied it there.

ALL OUR YESTERDAYS

I quite understand when I hear people say

Events long gone by seem like "just yesterday,"

But here's a conundrum I haven't solved yet —

What happened just yesterday? Guess what...I forget!

OBSOLESCENCE

He tells himself he's stopped to rest his feet.
The stubborn truth his tear-dimmed eyes impart:
That building coming down across the street
Contains his heart.

The demolition men should feel no guilt
For wrecking what was born within his brain,
Nor should we fault this man who had it built
For feeling pain.

There is no issue here of placing blame,
No question of defining right from wrong,
But wonderment: "Perhaps I've played the game
A bit too long."

He's lived enough to know what's past is past,
And yet it jolts his confidence to see
The death of this great structure built to last
A century.

The battered briefcase dangling from his hand—
Its leather worn, threads rotting at the seams—
Encloses the prospectus he has planned
To sell his dreams.

The strange new breed of broker he meets now
Who stride right in on those he waits to see—
Oh, how he'd love to show these youngsters how
It used to be.

To him New York was Eldorado then,
His faculties were keen, appearance trim,
And he knew all his era's builder men
And they knew him.

The doors of Gotham opened to his knock,
The heavy carpets gave beneath his tread.
Wise realtors attended and took stock
In what he said.

Square blocks, whole neighborhoods were his domain,
His vision, his persistence made them rise.
Perhaps he knows such days won't come again,
But still he tries.

Self-pity? No, he hasn't time for it,
For time is short, yet courage deep-instilled;
The fine assemblage he will now submit
Is one they'll build!

He's concentrated all his skills of old,
But, being out of touch, how would he know
The site that he will surely sell was sold
A week ago.

It was not always so. When in his prime,
Few matched his pace and fewer still would try,
That is, until the race was joined by time
Which passed him by.

While breath remains, he stubbornly competes;
For this old broker heaven must unfold
Its promise of a deal a day where streets
Are paved with gold.

RELATIVITY

That I have reached my 70s

Is no big deal I find,

But the fact that my daughter's now 46

Totally blows my mind.

BONUS TIME

Grandkids are our late-life bonus,
Heart and soul, it seems, they own us.
For all the deviltry that's in them,
It's not our job to discipline them,
Ah, no! That function's for their parents
While we show patience and forbearance.
Amused, we smile Cheshire-catly,
Years back we warned our children flatly:
"Wait! Just wait until you're grown
And you have children of your own!"
Our children barely paid attention
Nor showed the slightest apprehension,
And life evolved just as it should,
In time we reached grandparenthood.

Now, what a happy status this is:
Paradise with hugs and kisses!
And if perchance our grandkids act up
It isn't long before we're packed up
Ending this day's visitation,
But, what a win-win situation!
We've had the pure and simple pleasure
Of spending time with kids we treasure

Without a role in taking action
(Been there, done that) for each infraction.
The moment we are out the door,
Our son speaks words he'd heard before
Voiced in his own paternal tone:
"Wait! Just wait until you're grown…"

YOU'VE GOT TO KEEP THE BOY
IN THE MAN

Old buddies I grew up with get me down
When they get off from work and come to town.
The life they lead, it weighs a ton,
They have no time for having fun,
Instead they wear life's burdens like a crown.

They think this is the way it's got to be,
I let them know it's not the way for me.
I'll do the things I've always done
From way back then when I was young,
Just laughing up a storm and floating free.

I've put on weight and lost a little hair,
That surely is no reason for despair.
I'm clinging to the youthful ways
Of all my bygone youthful days
And if some folks don't like it, I don't care.

Some say I'm always acting like a child,
Forever fooling around and running wild,
I like the ladies, that's a fact,
I wink — and sometimes they wink back.
Staring at the wall is not my style.

You know, the boy is father to the man,
The boy I was, I want him close at hand.
I realize life's short enough,
So it makes sense to live it up,
You've got to keep the boy in the man.

You've got to keep the boy in the man,
You've got to keep the boy in the man,
For there's no way that I'm
Growing old before my time,
You've got to keep the boy in the man.

TIME FOR A CHANGE

While leafing through my copy of Roget's Thesaurus,
I found several expressions that, in fact, do nothing for us.
They stand out wherever words like "old" and "aging"
      are defined,
I would like them all deleted, if the editors don't mind.

For example, these three phrases all articulate that I'm
"Old as Methuselah," "old as the hills," and also "past
      my prime."
And, furthermore, here's "ripe old age" and there's
      "long in the tooth."
I'm sick and tired of the lot, and that's the living truth.

Though editors in general are good people, I suspect
They don't know the definition of "politically correct,"
If they did, they'd realize those old expressions should
      be lifted
For this one phrase that says it all…"Geriatrically-Gifted!"

LIKE FATHER, LIKE SON

I used to scoff at poppa

For the many pills he popped.

Poppa's gone, now I'm a popper, too

And I'm gonna keep on poppin'

Like my Poppa 'til I drop!

I'd opt to stop but that would not

Be quite the proper thing to do.

POOF!

No one really asked me,
But if somebody had,
I would have made him realize
The system's pretty bad:
What sense is there in climbing
Half a life to reach a peak,
Then sliding down the other half
Until we're old and weak?

There's got to be a better way,
(Old age is ample proof)
That better way on our fated day
Is to just...go...
POOF!

Both physically and mentally
A man should hit his prime,
And stick around in comfort
'Til his predetermined time.
Then at 23 or 93
Or somewhere in between,
A little poof, a puff of smoke,
And he's no longer seen.

There's got to be a better way,
(I say we raise the roof!)
That better way on our fated day
Is to just…go…
POOF!

If we gotta go, we gotta go,
But someone tell me why
There shouldn't be a better way
To kiss the world goodbye.
The way things are, the final joke's
On us. Oh, what a goof!
Now, what's wrong with a puff of smoke,
A non-polluting puff of smoke,
A final, fleeting puff of smoke
As we…go…
POOF!

MISSION ACCOMPLISHED

When I think back to way-back-when,
(The boy I was had just turned ten),
I daydreamed I might live to see
The birth of a new century;
This also meant the time had come
To welcome the millenium
Plus my own 70th year on earth!
(Talk about getting your money's worth!)
But, this trifecta... truth be told,
I seriously doubted would unfold,
Six decades distant, after all,
Seems like forever when you're small,
But years, then decades came and went,
My time was by and large well-spent,
Despite life's worries to subdue
And myriad minefields to pass through.

I'm thankful I did not succumb
Before the new millennium,
The trouble is — it's sad to say —
I had become a tad blasé
2001...2002...
Have come and gone. What else is new?

2003? Each boring dawn
Now finds me waking with a yawn.
The future, with its dullish cast,
Becomes the present, then the past.
I learn as each new day arrives
I cannot live my children's lives,
It's obvious I should have known
That they have missions of their own.
As for the grandkids, bless their souls,
They're playing out their childhood roles.
I love my big and little heirs,
But I have my life, they have theirs.
I need another mission…bad!
To help replace the one I had.

What other goal might I now set
That has a chance of being met?
The 22nd century?
No, that's too big a reach for me,
To live so long would be no good,
I wouldn't want to if I could.
Perhaps 100 years all told?
Not bad, for I'd be pigeon-holed
With centenarians who are
The fastest-growing group by far,
(That is to say, percentage-wise,
I've seen the charts with my own eyes).

The odds are anything but short,
One in 10,000, at last report,
But that just proves it can be done;
No matter what, it's worth the run.
With 27 years to go...
The outcome? Hey! You never know.
Though 2030's not that near,
With any luck, I'll see you there.

A TOAST

We've ridden that old roller coaster called life,

We've known all the ups and the downs.

Sometimes we've acted like kings and like queens

And sometimes we've acted like clowns.

Here's to our lives and the parts that we played

Here's to our family and friends,

Here's to our place in the human parade,

Let's enjoy the parade 'til it ends.

THE UNIVERSE

I wasn't there at the very start of it,

But I'm grateful to have been a part of it.

PREVIOUSLY PUBLISHED

"I'd Like You to Meet..." *Public Employees News (PEN)*, 1974

The following poems were originally published in *Realty* between 1964 and 1971 and republished in the book, <u>The Reluctant Investor and Other Light Verse</u> by Don Weill, Copyright 1977, The Eldon Press: "Dialog," "Obsolescence," "Remember Babylonia" and "The Reluctant Investor."

"Full Circle" *Grit*, 1980

The following poems originally appeared in the *Metropolitan Diary* section of the *New York Times*, Copyright by the New York Times Co. and reprinted by permission: "A Star Too Far" 1999, "Lost at the Beach" 2001, "Shhh...," "The Negotiator" and "Who, What, When, Where" 2002.

"Role Model" *Sarasota Herald-Tribune*, 2003
Super Senior Tennis News, 2003

ACKNOWLEDGMENTS

I extend my gratitude to the following people for their assistance in this endeavor:

My wife Elaine who served as a sounding board for the meter and rhyme, the wording and the phrasing of many of these poems;

My late father, Wilford Weill, novelist, short story and light verse writer, for introducing me to the joys of humorous verse when I was very, very young;

Daughter Wendi, without whom this book would never have seen the light of day. She has guided this effort from the very beginning;

Son Steve and daughter-in-law Sabrina for their editorial, grammatical and photographic assistance, and for introducing me to the Computer Age;

Son-in-law Matt for lending the support of his agency, the Seiden Group, particularly Jessica Venegas who contributed mightily to the design and production of this book;

Son Jeff and daughter-in-law Julie and son Kenny and daughter-in-law Joanna for their steadfast encouragement;

Stephen L. DeFelice, M.D., author of <u>Old Italian Neighborhood Values</u>, a novel, for his ongoing suggestions on publishing and promoting that which has been published;

Irwin Becker, M.D. for his insights on the annual physical examination described in "Doctor, No Surprises, Please";

Esther Gordon for her generous advice during the early days of this project;

Hank Seiden for the joke on which "The Joke" is based;

Jim Brown, columnist for the *Sarasota Herald-Tribune*, for "nominating" me as poet laureate of Longboat Key.

ABOUT THE AUTHOR...

Don Weill retired eight years ago from a long career as a broker and investor in Lower Manhattan real estate. In his distant youth, he was editor of the Syracuse University *Daily Orange* and class poet laureate. Following two-year's service during the Korean War, he worked as a reporter-rewrite man for the *Long Island Star-Journal* and then published a small daily newspaper in Somerville, N.J., *The Somerset Star.* A lifelong versifier, his poems have appeared in *The Saturday Evening Post, The New York Times, The Wall Street Journal* and other publications. He is the author of <u>The Reluctant Investor and Other Light Verse</u> published in 1977, a collection of his real estate poems which had appeared in *Realty* over the previous fifteen years. Father of four and grandfather of six with two more on the way, he resides in Westfield, N.J. with his wife Elaine. They spend long summer weekends on Long Beach Island, N.J. and long winter months on Longboat Key, Fl.

Printed in the United States
21382LVS00001B/34-108

9 781418 409746